You've Written Your Book. Now What?

A Self-Publishing Guide for Entrepreneurs

Deborah Kevin

HIGHLANDER PRESS

Copyright© 2020 by Highlander Enterprises, LLC

Printed in the United States of America

All Rights Reserved. No part of this book may be reproduced in any form or by any means without written permission from the author or publisher except for brief quotations embodied in critical essay, article, or review. These articles and/or views must state the correct title and contributing author of this book by name.

Limit of Liability/Disclaimer of Warranty: While the publisher and the author have used their best efforts in preparing this book, they make no representations or warranties with respect to accuracy or completeness of the contents of this book and specifically disclaim any implied warranties of merchantability or fitness for a particular purpose. No warranty may be created or extended by sales representatives or written sales materials. The advice and strategies contained herein may not be suitable for your situation. You should consult with a professional where appropriate. Neither the publisher nor the author shall be liable for any loss of profit or any other commercial damages, including but not limited to special, incidental, consequential, or other damages.

Earnings Disclaimer: The publisher and author make no implications, warranties, promises, suggestions, projections, representations, or guarantees with respect to future prospects or earnings. There is no assurance that any prior successes or past results as to earnings or income results will apply, nor can any prior success be used as an indication of your future successes or results from any of the information, content, or strategies.

Published by: Highlander Press

Editor: Deborah Kevin

Cover Design: Hanne Brøter, Your Brand Vision

Layout: Catherine Williams, Chapter One Book Production

Author Photo: Brenda Jankowski

ISBN 978-1-7343764-5-6

To my sons, Cooper and Jack,
I love you to infinity and beyond.

Table of Contents

Introduction 1
Book Basics 3
Hire an Editor 7
Decide How You Want to Publish 11
Design Your Cover 15
Book Layout 19
Categories, Keywords and Pricing—Oh My! 22
Proofread Your Book 25
Final Revisions 27
Publish and Celebrate! 29
Getting Eyeballs on Your Book 30
Wrapping It Up 32
Resources 33
Acknowledgments 34
About the Author 37

Introduction

Before we go into your next steps, I invite you to pause right now and celebrate the freakin' fantastic accomplishment of having written a book! Most authors I know tend to focus on the "now what" and forget to *celebrate each step* of the process. And, having kept your commitment to getting your book written is worthy of celebration. So, cheers!

Now the bad news. What you've written is the first draft—the first of many drafts. Don't be discouraged—you're among the greats—like Hemingway, Wolfe, Shakespeare—who loved revision. Why? Think of it this way: your first draft is the raw marble block from which you, like Michaelangelo, will care a beautiful piece of art. While the marble itself is striking, it can't compare to the final product.

You may be scratching your head about now, wondering, "This feels so much bigger than I thought." I'm not gonna lie to you: it is. But I've got you! This guidebook will walk you through what steps will take you from the first draft to becoming a published author. Before jumping into each action outlined in this book, I suggest you first read through the entire book so you can globally understand what's in front of you.

While much of this guidebook will help you do things yourself, there are a few crucial skills where you will want to invest so that your book can be a full representation of your brilliance. They are professional editing, graphic design, and book layout.

Let's do this!

Book Basics

Regardless of how your book is published, there are general guidelines that will support your longer-term goal of becoming an author. Adhering to these principles will help you, your designer, and your publisher (even if that's you!) edit and publish your best book. In this chapter, we'll explore typical book lengths, types of books, and submission best practices.

Book Length

One question that often comes up when talking with entrepreneurs about their books is, "How long should my book be?" My response is, "That depends on what the goal is for your book." I realize that's not a helpful answer, so I've created a chart to provide rough word counts and the number 8.5 x 11 pages (most books are ultimately published as 6 x 9, but are written in 8.5 x 11). Keep in mind that they are averages, not set-in-stone absolutes.

These are rough numbers based upon the following assumptions:

- Double-spaced text
- One-inch margins
- 12-point font

Book Type	Avg. Word Count	Avg. No. of Pages	Publish
Freebie	1,500-2,500	6-10	PDF on website
Expert-Level	20,000	80	Self or Hybrid
Thought Leader	75,000	300	Self, Hybrid, Traditional
How-To	50,000	200	Self or Hybrid
Memoir	60,000	240	Self, Hybrid, Traditional
Fiction (adult)	80,000	320	Self, Hybrid, Traditional
Fiction (young adult)	70,000	280	Self, Hybrid, Traditional
Fiction (middle grade)	50,000	200	Self, Hybrid, Traditional

Types of Books

Let's explore the differences between Freebie, Expert-Level, Thought Leader, and How-To books.

- **Freebie.** This document is created to entice your potential clients to download something of value in exchange for their email addresses. Freebies live on your website and are integrated with your email service. Best practices include numbered pages and conversion to a PDF.

- **Expert-Level.** An expert-level book is a more substantive version of a freebie, and it is designed to establish one's expertise in a particular area. It's written to solve a specific problem that your clients experience. This book is an excellent example of an expert-level book. These kinds of books are typically self-published or published through a hybrid publisher.

- **Thought Leader.** A thought leader book is significantly more substantive than an expert-level book. It delves deeply into processes or ideas and provides meaningful guidance to your readers. Because these books are heftier, you may be able to publish via a traditional publisher. More likely, though, is that you'll either self-publish or go through a hybrid press.

- **How-To.** A how-to book is one the focuses on helping your readers accomplish a task or process. Perhaps you've created a unique way of achieving something and want to share your knowledge with others. This book is an example of combining a how-to with an expert-level book. These kinds of books are typically self-published or published through a hybrid publisher.

Submission Best Practices
Each publisher has its own submission guidelines, so these general rules of thumb are offered as best practices, especially useful for self-publishing.

- Number your pages
- Double-space your text
- Use a 12-point font
- Use your branded fonts if you have them. Otherwise, use Times Roman or Courier.
- Set your margins to mirror each other
- Begin new chapters or sections on odd page numbers

Now that we have the basics out of the way let's delve into how to publish your book.

Hire an Editor

Editing is one area in which many self-published authors fail. They either edit the book themselves, get a friend to do the editing, or—worst of all—publish their first draft. It's precisely these authors who give self-publishing a bad rap. And we don't want that for you.

Before we get into how to select the right editor for your work, it's essential to understand that there are several different kinds of editing, and they're not interchangeable.

- **Developmental editor.** This editor looks at the big picture. Does your book work? Are you using all the story elements appropriately (yes, even nonfiction books use story elements)? Feedback from this editor will strengthen your overall book, whether it's a novel or nonfiction.

- **Line editor.** A line editor will provide a comprehensive critique that includes developmental structure, word choice, writing style, and language.

- **Copyeditor.** A copyeditor could also be called the grammar and punctuation police! This editor also ensures consistency of spelling and terminology throughout your book.

- **Proofreader.** Once your book has been set-up in InDesign and uploaded, a proofreader gives your book a last once over to ensure that there's nothing funky going on (like missing pages or paragraph truncation—because I know from experience that this happens!).

That being said, not all editors are created equal. A great editor is a combination of wicked grammar skills, knowledge, and intuition. Your editor will be all up in your business, so developing a trusting rapport is crucial to having your best work brought forth. I hear you say, "That's great, but how do I know if an editor is right for me?"

I'm glad you asked. Here are my recommendations:

1. **Make a list of characteristics of someone with whom you could work well.**
   If you're a Type A personality, you might not want someone who is Bohemian. Schedules not your jam? Perhaps stay away from a high-pressure editor. Is a sense of humor important to you? Is having a specific outlook?

2. **Ask others who they used—and loved.**
   Recommendations are great to receive because you can ask detailed questions about the editing process and figure out what works for you. Chances are if someone

you know, like, and trust had an editor they loved, you'll likely be a good fit, too.

3. **Research.**

   Check out lists like Editorial Freelance Association or Upwork. Gather a few names and research the books they've edited. Were the books well received? What kind of reviews were there?

4. **Interview.**

   Once you've narrowed down your list to a few candidates, schedule a call with them. You'll want to ask these questions:

   - What kind of services do they offer?
   - What's their turnaround time?
   - When are they available
   - What other projects have they worked on?
   - Can you call a couple of their past clients?
   - What is your investment, and how can you structure payment?

5. **Assess.**

   Most professional editors will ask you to submit a book summary and the first ten pages of your book for them to assess. This assessment will result in both inline edits made directly to your manuscript as well as an editorial letter, which ought to highlight what's brilliant about your work and their assessment of what the editing project will entail. This review is essential for you to determine if the editor is right for you—and for them to assess if you're right for them. The bottom line is that you want a skillful editor who will tenderly and honestly support you as an author.

6. **Select one with whom you feel comfortable.**
   Hopefully, you found an editor who respected the tone of voice of your work, skillfully provided critical feedback, and carefully corrected grammatical errors. If not, don't be afraid to begin again. Once you have your dream editor, sign a contract, make your deposit, and trust that you made a great decision.

Decide How You Want to Publish

This guidebook is specifically for authors who want to self-publish. That being said, I would be remiss if I didn't explain the various ways you can publish your book. There are three main avenues for authors to become published: self-publishing, hybrid publishing, and traditional publishing. Let's explore the similarities and differences.

Features	Self	Hybrid	Traditional
Control over layout & cover	Most	Moderate	Least
Copyright holder	You	You	Publisher
Author marketing efforts	100%	75%	80%
Author royalty, on average	100%	80%	20%
Author Investment	Yes	Yes	No
Author advance	No	No	Possibly
Publishing back-end set-up	Author	Publisher	Publisher
Select publishing categories	Author	Publisher w/ Author	Publisher
Select pricing	Author	Publisher w/ Author	Publisher
Draft to publication timeframe	Short	9-12 months	2+ years
Select publication date	Author	Publisher	Publisher

Traditional publishing has long been considered the pinnacle of an author's dream. But gone are the days of significant advances, publisher-funded book tours, and extensive marketing. The traditional publishing process typically takes at least two years, during which time the following occurs:

- Author secures an agent
- The agent auctions the book
- Publishing houses bid
- Winner licenses the book's copyright
- An editor is assigned
- Revisions are made
- Book cover and interior are designed
- Book is pre-pubbed
- Book is launched

What some people don't realize is that even after your book is agented, it may not sell at auction because it doesn't fit any publishers' catalog of needs.

Hybrid publishers are typically boutique presses. They're smaller, more nimble, and look to publish specific kinds of books. Hybrid presses range from vanity presses, who will—for a fee—publish anyone's book regardless of its quality, to niche presses, who specialize in romance, science fiction, literary fiction, or nonfiction. Hybrid presses often require the author to make an investment to cover editing, design, and marketing costs, and this fee can range anywhere from $10,000 to $25,000, depending on how much editing is required as well as book complexity. Legitimate hybrid presses, which are on the upswing, can be researched on the Independent Book Publisher's Association website (https://www.ibpa-online.org/).

Self-publishing, although most people immediately think of Amazon, can occur on any number of platforms. The benefit of self-publishing is that you get to make all the decisions about how and when to publish your book. Of course, this is also bad news as you may not know how to put your book forward in the best light by selecting the right categories or keywords, which are crucial for any self-publishing venture.

When selecting where to self-publish, you'll want to look at where you're going to get the most exposure and distribution. Most authors immediately think of publishing their books directly on Amazon via their proprietary KDP platform. And, for many, this may be perfect. Others may want broader exposure than Amazon can give them, or they may wish for their hometown bookstore to carry their masterpiece.

Let's compare Amazon-KDP to another self-publishing tool called IngramSpark.

Features	Amazon-KDP	IngramSpark
Global distribution	Yes	Yes
Local & online bookstores	No	Yes
Available on Amazon?	Yes	Yes
ISBN	Free, included*	Purchase
Hardback available?	No	Yes
Paperback available?	Yes	Yes
eBook available?	Yes	Yes
Cost to publish	Free	Between $25-49
Author purchase pricing?	Yes	Yes
Layout requirements	KDP template	InDesign layout
Cover requirements	KDP template	IngramSpark template
Royalties paid	90-days after month, direct deposit	90-days after month, direct deposit

* Note that if you use Amazon's free ISBN, you are obligated to publish through them as they own the ISBN. It's a best practice to purchase your own ISBN and use it on whatever platform you choose.

Some self-publishing authors use both Amazon KDP and IngramSpark, maximizing their distribution options. That sophisticated option goes beyond this simple guidebook.

Design Your Cover

The cover design is one area where investing in a graphic design professional makes sense. Sure, you could fire up Canva and use one of their templates, and you'd be fine. Just ask yourself, "Is 'fine' the feeling I'm going for?" And since sometimes you *can* tell a book by its cover, do yourself a favor and hire an experienced book designer.

I often get asked, "How do I know how to decide what my cover ought to look like?" First, consider browsing your local or online bookstore. What covers grab your attention—and why? Are there covers you don't like? What about them repels you?

If you're so inclined, create a Pinterest board to capture things you like: colors, patterns, book covers, accessories, clothing, and inspirational quotes. Having a broad view of your aesthetic will help your designer create a book cover that speaks to you—and your ideal clients. For example, if you have a Bohemian style, your book cover ought not to be styled like Ralph Lauren.

If you're using Amazon or IngramSpark (or another printer and distributor), you can download their book cover templates and share them with your designer. You'll be asked the number of pages, book size, and a few other questions so your unique template can be created. Note that I estimate the number of pages to allow the graphic designer to begin work on the book before it's finished with the editing process. Once the final numbers are known, the cover can be tweaked before finalized for uploading.

Cover Inputs

Regardless of what your cover ultimately looks like, there are several standard inputs. They are:

- Your branding style guide (colors, fonts, and logo)
- A summary for the back cover
- Blurbs (optional)
- A 50-word author biography
- A professional author headshot
- ISBN

Let's dig a little into the summary, blurbs, biography, and ISBN.

Summary

If the cover of your book captures someone's eye and the title entices them to select it, it's the summary that closes the deal. A compelling summary is relatively short, crisp, and clear. When crafting your book summary, consider all the places it will be seen. First, the summary appears at the top of the back cover, where it will help browsers decide if your book is for them. The overview also appears on any site where your book will be sold, like Amazon, Barnes & Noble, Powell's, or others.

Blurbs

Blurbs are the testimonials, or social proof, for your book. If you opt to obtain blurbs, select one (two at most) of the most influential blurbs for your back cover—this means no relatives or besties! To maximize their impact, select blurbs that complement each other rather than two that say the same thing.

Author Biography

Every entrepreneur ought to have at her fingertips three biographies: a long-form version, a 100-word version, and a 50-word version. If you don't, stop reading and write your long-form biography. Here's the most crucial aspect of any of your bios—it ought not to be a version of your resume (that's what LinkedIn is for). Your bios ought to capture your "Why"—thank you, Simon Sinek—and your personality. People work with those they know, like, and trust. Let your freak flag fly in your authentic bio.

ISBN

In the previous chapter, we touched briefly on the ISBN, or International Standard Book Number. The ISBN is a numeric commercial book identifier, which can be purchased from an affiliate of the International ISBN Agency. An ISBN is assigned to each separate edition and variation of a publication (you'll need one for every version of your book you plan to publish: hardback, paperback, ebook, and audiobook).

Again, purchasing your own ISBN is a worthwhile investment. I believe it's a disservice to authors to use the free Amazon ISBN as this forever limits where and how they can publish their book. I use a service called Bowker (http://www.bowker.com/).

Sometimes I get asked if one ought to purchase the ISBN and barcode. If you want your book to be scannable at your local bookshop, then buying a barcode is a wise decision. If funds are tight, you can forego the barcode.

Book Layout

The way your book looks in print is due to the brilliance of a specialized graphic designer who works with interior book layouts. The designer takes into account your branding, which includes colors and fonts, as well as your aesthetic and readers you're looking to attract. Other considerations include pagination, image layout, and section breaks.

Let's look at the anatomy of a book, so you can visualize each of the sections—and support your graphic designer to increase efficiency. Where you've likely spent the majority of your time is in the text or body of your book. If you've done research, you may also have comprehensive appendices, indexes, or endnotes.

- Front Matter
    - Title page
    - Other Works (optional)
    - Colophon or Copyright details
    - Dedication or Epigram
    - Table of Contents
    - Foreword (optional)

- Text or Body
  - Introduction
  - Chapters

- Back Matter
  - Appendices, Index, or Endnotes (optional)
  - Acknowledgments
  - Author Biography
  - Reader Guide (optional)

As you can see, hiring a professional to design and layout your book will be an investment that reaps many rewards!

The front matter section typically is numbered with Roman numerals. The title page, although the first page in this section, ought not to have the number printed (e.g., usually, the copyright page would be page ii).

The back matter section continues the body section numbering unless you have heavy references, in which case you might choose a differing page numbering scheme.

If you pull a book off your shelf, you'll also notice that the pages are mirrored, which accounts for the binding space. The left-facing and right-facing page headers are different as well. One contains the author's name and the other the book title.

These complexities are why I highly recommend using a book layout expert to design your book in InDesign rather than using the glitchy KDP templates. Should you use the KDP templates, you'll want to familiarize yourself with advanced Word functions like sections, section breaks, numbering, and references.

A note on using an InDesign expert: IngramSpark requires their books to be laid out in InDesign, whereas KDP does not. I recommend InDesign regardless of how you'll self-publish if only to eliminate having to become a Word expert and pull your hair out over templates with wonky coding.

Categories, Keywords, and Pricing—Oh, My!

Metadata, otherwise known as publishing categories, keywords, and pricing, is often overlooked by the self-published author. Yet, it is metadata that makes it easy to find your book in a search. Plan on spending *at least* a full day researching the best categories, keywords, and pricing for your book. Skip this work at your peril! An extremely useful tool to aid in this research is KDPRocket, which can be used regardless of which platform(s) you're using to publish your book.

Let's dig into each area.

Publishing Categories
Publishing categories are also known as BISAC codes, which make it easy to determine what your book is about. BISAC codes identify your primary genre(s), topic(s), and theme(s), and are used by book retailers and resellers to categorize your book. I suggest that you choose three, but you're required to select at least one.

The first code you select will be the primary category where your book can be found. If you're not sure where to begin, I suggest visiting good ol' Amazon and searching for books that you feel are similar to yours. Scroll down to the bottom, and you'll find the publishing details, which include the book's categories.

Use the BISAC list (https://bisg.org/page/BISACEdition) and choose your top three. These codes will be used in any of your publishing platforms back-end set-ups.

Keywords

Keywords for books are similar to SEO keywords in that they can be single words or phrases. How you can think about keywords is pretty simple. What would your ideal reader type into the Google search bar to find your book? KDPRocket is a handy dandy tool for identifying powerful keywords.

Pricing

One question that authors always ask me is, "What should I charge for my book?" The best way to figure out that answer is research. When I work with my authors, I research at least ten books that fall into similar categories. I create a spreadsheet to catalog book titles, the authors, number of pages, dates published, pricing, keywords, and categories. I run an average of what the books are priced at, compare mine in content and size, and then set a draft price. I say draft because until you're in the final stages of book set-up in KDP, you won't know what the minimum amount is as required by KDP/Amazon to cover printing costs.

Metadata

Once you've completed this research, and determined what categories, keywords, and pricing your book will have, you've got the metadata figured out. Hurrah! This information will be uploaded into your self-publishing account as part of your book set-up.

Proofread Your Book

We touched briefly on proofreading earlier in this book when we explained the various types of editing you'd need. Proofreading is that final bastion between you and a box of misprinted books (yes, I'm speaking from experience!). Once your book is uploaded onto the platform(s) you've selected, order a paper proof copy. Yes, it extends the "go-live" date by a couple of weeks, but it is entirely worth the time.

Once you have a printed book in your hand (whoa! Celebrate that moment!), pour your favorite beverage and sit in your coziest chair and read your book, cover to cover. Now isn't the time to be questioning the content. It is the time, however, to look for widows and orphans (single lines of text on a page), alignment, continuity, and accuracy.

Have more than one proofreader, if you can. True story: one of the books I published was proofed by the author, his wife, his mother, and her sister before being signed off as approved. When the books arrived at his home in advance of an event—3,000 of them—there were pages out of sequence. When we discovered the error, one of the proofreaders said, "Yeah, I noticed that, but I didn't want to upset you." *Slaps forehead* Trust me, it's *way* more upsetting to receive 3,000 books that are misprinted. Not to mention hella expensive to replace them.

Final Revisions

Once you've completed the proofreading stage, you'll likely have a few corrections to make in your final document. Make those adjustments, save your file, and note it as the FINAL copy. Convert it to a PDF and upload it to KDP or IngramSpark.

Both Amazon and IngramSpark processing and review takes a few days, after which you'll either receive a notification that the book is reading for a second proof or there are additional issues to be resolved. If there are issues to fix, do that before continuing.

Once the book is ready for final proofing, you have a choice: review the document online or order a second proof copy. It's best practice to review an actual book, but sometimes timing is such that an online review works for the final product.

A word of caution here: you can stay in the proofing-review-updating loop for eternity and never wholly fix all the issues in your book. Your goal ought to be accuracy over perfection. A reader who is transfixed by your message in your well-crafted and well-edited book won't judge you for one or two minor mistakes. They will judge you and lose faith in your expertise for a slapdash edition, though.

Here's how I get comfortable with the odd typo or misplaced comma: the Persians who hand-knot their gorgeous rugs add in one imperfection because they believe only God (or whatever name you assign to a higher energy or being) is perfect. If unique rugs costings thousands of dollars can be imperfect, so can your self-published book!

Publish and Celebrate!

Before you push the "publish" button, I invite you to pause. Reflect on all the work that has brought you to this moment. Feel the gratitude for all the support and encouragement you received throughout the entire process.

Then, and only then, press the "publish" button.

Congratulations! You're now a self-published author. Be sure to break open the champagne or sparkling cider and toast to your monumental achievement!

Getting Eyeballs on Your Book

Well, you've done it! You published the best book you possibly could. You're watching your book like a hawk on Amazon or Barnes & Noble to see who's purchasing and reading and reviewing your book. Unfortunately, it feels like watching paint dry.

Here's another area where most authors underestimate the time and effort to get eyeballs on their books: marketing. Unfortunately, this isn't a case of "write it, and they will read" à la *The Field of Dreams*. You'll want to develop and execute a marketing plan. In truth, your marketing plan ought to be started *at least* six weeks before your book is published.

While this book won't delve deeply into marketing your book, here are a few marketing tasks to consider:

- Hold online and in-person launch parties (not on the same day)
- Write an electronic press kit (EPK), post it on your website

- Send a press release to your local media outlets
- Develop a signature presentation based upon your book and deliver it
- Have a social media campaign that includes all outlets you use
- Ask your network for support in sharing the good news that your book is out
- Send a warm letter to all your contacts, announcing your good news
- Host readings, online or in-person
- Ask for Amazon reviews
- Be sure to create your Amazon author page via Author Central (https://authorcentral.amazon.com/) and link your book to that account
- Look for podcasts on which you can be an expert guest
- Add a link to your email signature block that sends people to your Amazon book page

Some specialists regularly conduct book launches for authors. If marketing your book feels daunting, you may want to consider hiring an online book launch specialist.

If your goal is to garner media coverage, investing in a public relations (PR) professional is worth its weight in gold. A seasoned PR person has media connections and keeps her thumb on the pulse of the community. She can quickly respond to those who want someone with your expertise. And with journalists, speed of response and relationships are two critical factors in achieving success. Just know that using PR is a long game tactic, and you get from it what you invest.

Wrapping It Up

I hope you've found this guide to self-publishing incredibly helpful and that your book is successfully written, edited, designed, proofed, and published, so it creates the ripple effect of change in a world that so desperately needs it.

If, after reading through this book, you decide you'd like to hand over the publishing, launching, and publicizing of your book to a professional, you're invited to submit a query via my website https://www.highanderpressbooks.com. If we're not a good fit for publication, I will happily connect you with other respected industry professionals who could serve you.

Resources

This list includes some of my favorite editing, researching, publishing, and launching tools.

- *The Chicago Manual of Style*
- *The Elements of Style* by Strunk and White
- KDPRocket
- Grammarly
- PerfectIt
- Evernote
- IngramSpark
- Draft2Digital
- Amazon KDP

The following resources are available on the Highlander Press website (https://www.highlanderpressbooks.com):

- What Kind of Editor Do You Need?
- 7 Questions to Ask Before Hiring an Editor
- 12 Ways to Strengthen Your Writing
- Get Noticed! Electronic Press Kit Guide

Acknowledgments

It takes a village to bring a book to life, and I'm blessed with the most remarkable village of all.

Thank you to Hanne Brøter of Your Brand Vision, who created the Highlander Press logo and this book's cover, along with my website and marketing collateral. She's not only a gifted designer but an excellent teacher and even better friend.

Catherine Williams is my go-to for InDesign. I'm forever grateful that she reached out to introduce herself. Her expertise and wisdom are blessings. I couldn't wait to present her with my book for layout because I knew it would be beautiful. I was right!

To Connie Jo Miller, my sister from another mister, who has been a long-time friend and cheerleader, I love you. Your humor and counsel are priceless to me, and I'm forever grateful for that day you sauntered into Kodak's open space and my life.

To my 100-day Mastermind powerhouses, Nicole Meltzer, Jill Celeste, Clare Whalley, Carrie Ekins, and Jen Kline Clark, for nudging me to step out fully as a publisher and book expert. Your questions helped me identify where I wanted to spend my time, and you provided a safe place to practice. I wouldn't want to do this entrepreneurial life without you in my corner.

To my sons Cooper and Jack, for trusting me to support our little family unconventionally. When times were lean, and I felt discouraged, you wouldn't let me give up and pursue an easier path. I'm so proud to be your mom. Thank you for believing in me and for the great hugs!

Lastly, to Princess Leia and Fergus, for sitting on my lap or at my feet as I wrote and edited. You ought to receive co-creator credits. Thank you for reminding me to play every day!

About the Author

Deborah Kevin (pronounced "KEY-vin"), the founder and Chief Inspiration Officer* of Highlander Press, loves books. Since teaching herself to read when she was four years old until now, books have been her constant companions.

A writer herself, she enjoys guiding others through the process of writing, editing, and publishing their books. Her clients have said they feel held and supported through the process of becoming bestselling authors, and they realized that Deborah saw something in their words that others missed.

Ms. Kevin lives with her family in Baltimore City, Maryland, with a pup named Fergus—that is, when they're not off discovering the world. You can follow her and Highlander Press on social media.

Learn more by visiting https://www.highanderpressbooks.com.

---

*One of the joys of being self-employed is that one can assign whatever title one desires!

www.ingramcontent.com/pod-product-compliance
Lightning Source LLC
Chambersburg PA
CBHW051040030426
42336CB00015B/2968